Playing Fair

Katie Peters

GRL Consultants,
Diane Craig and Monica Marx,
Certified Literacy Specialists

Pull Ahead Readers People Smarts

Lerner Publications ◆ Minneapolis

Note from a GRL Consultant
This Pull Ahead leveled book has been carefully designed for beginning readers. A team of guided reading literacy experts has reviewed and leveled the book to ensure readers pull ahead and experience success.

Lerner Publications Company
An imprint of Lerner Publishing Group, Inc.
241 First Avenue North
Minneapolis, MN 55401 USA

For reading levels and more information, look up this title at www.lernerbooks.com.

Main body text set in Memphis Pro 24/39
Typeface provided by Linotype

Photo Acknowledgments
The images in this book are used with the permission of: © artisteer/Getty Images, p. 3; © FatCamera/Getty Images, pp. 14–15; © fstop123/Getty Images, pp. 8–9; © Jeff Greenough/Getty Images, pp. 6–7; © Marilyn Nieves/Getty Images, pp. 10–11, 16 (right); © recep-bg/Getty Images, pp. 12–13, 16 (left); © SDI Productions/Getty Images, pp. 4–5, 16 (center).

Front cover: © SerrNovik/Getty Images.

Library of Congress Cataloging-in-Publication Data

Names: Peters, Katie, author.
Title: Playing fair / Katie Peters.
Description: Minneapolis : Lerner Publications, 2022. | Series: Be a good sport. Pull ahead readers. People smarts. Nonfiction | Includes index. | Audience: Ages 4–7 | Audience: Grades K–1 | Summary: "What does it mean to play fair? Following rules, helping others, and taking turns are just a few examples. Pairs with the fiction title Your Turn"— Provided by publisher.
Identifiers: LCCN 2021010305 (print) | LCCN 2021010306 (ebook) | ISBN 9781728440927 (library binding) | ISBN 9781728444444 (ebook)
Subjects: LCSH: Sportsmanship—Juvenile literature.
Classification: LCC GV706.3 .P464 2022 (print) | LCC GV706.3 (ebook) | DDC 175—dc23

LC record available at https://lccn.loc.gov/2021010305
LC ebook record available at https://lccn.loc.gov/2021010306

Manufactured in the United States of America
1 – CG – 12/15/21

Table of Contents

Playing Fair

I know how to play fair.
I share the toys.

I know how to play fair.

I follow the rules.

I like to play fair.

I will wait for my turn.

I know how to play fair.
I let my sister have a turn.

I can play fair.

I help my brother play.

I know many ways
to play fair.

What is a way you can play fairly with your friends?

Did You See It?

bat

blocks

swing

Index